OF MICE AND MEN

NOTES

including

- *Life and Background*
- *List of Characters*
- *General Plot Summary*
- *Chapter Summaries and Commentaries*
- *General Meaning*
- *Character Analyses*
- *Structure and Style*
- *Questions for Review*
- *Bibliography*

by
James L. Roberts, Ph.D.
Department of English
University of Nebraska

Cliffs Notes

INCORPORATED

LINCOLN, NEBRASKA 68501

Editor

Gary Carey, M.A.
University of Colorado

Consulting Editor

James L. Roberts, Ph.D.
Department of English
University of Nebraska

Cliffs Notes, Inc.   Lincoln, Nebraska

CONTENTS

Of Mice and Men

LIFE AND BACKGROUND

John Steinbeck is the type of author who likes to know his material firsthand. He is not content to narrate a story which has no basis in fact. Thus many of his works take place in California and deal with subjects which he thoroughly understands. One of the finest attributes of *Of Mice and Men* is the feeling that the author knows his material and his characters in great depth and with perfect accuracy. The scenes in this novel, such as the episode in the bunkhouse, are narrated with the skill of a person who has witnessed the events.

Steinbeck's father settled in California shortly after the American Civil War. John Steinbeck was born in Salinas on February 27, 1902. His mother was a schoolteacher in the public school in Salinas. Steinbeck grew up in this beautiful, fertile California valley where he found the materials for most of his novels. His imagination was kindled by writing at a very early age partly because his mother, the schoolteacher, read to him from the famous literature of the world.

During his formative years, he played various sports in high school, worked at many different jobs, and wandered around the countryside observing the phenomena of nature. He entered Stanford University in 1920, and even though he remained until 1925, he never graduated. While in college, he attempted some creative writing which was submitted to magazines and was rejected. Not caring to complete the requirements for a degree and hoping to earn a living as an author, he left Stanford permanently in 1925 to live in New York. While writing and receiving rejection slips, he worked briefly for the old New York *American* newspaper and as a laborer on the construction of Madison Square Garden before returning to California. His first book, *Cup of Gold,* appeared in 1929 two months before the stock market crash and sold some fifteen hundred copies.

In two respects, 1930 was a notable year for Steinbeck: He married Carol Henning and the newlyweds settled in staid Pacific Grove which he often satirized. There, Steinbeck met Ed Ricketts, whose friendship strongly influenced Steinbeck's work. Ricketts, owner of a biological supply laboratory on Monterey's Cannery Row, became the hero of "The Snake," *Cannery Row,* and *Sweet Thursday,* as well as a collaborator in writing *The Sea of Cortez.*

During the era of "The Hungry Thirties"—a time of national depression, bread lines, and bloody, labor-management conflicts—Steinbeck knew a definitive cross-section of society and shared the problems and stresses of the times. His father, like many, miraculously helped the family to survive the depression with a small house and twenty-five dollars a month. Steinbeck continued his writing and received four hundred dollars for the first of his California novels, *The Pastures of Heaven* (1932). In 1933, *To a God Unknown,* a complicated, unsuccessful allegory, failed to repay the publisher's two-hundred-and-fifty dollar advance. Both publishers declared bankruptcy. That same year *North American Review* bought the first two parts of *The Red Pony* and some short stories, including "Murder," which was selected as an O. Henry Prize story for 1934 and brought Steinbeck his first national recognition.

Tortilla Flat (1935) was an immediate popular success and won the Gold Medal of the Commonwealth Club of San Francisco as the year's best novel by a Californian, even though critics missed the point of the droll humor about the unemployed drifters of Monterey. Steinbeck received three or four thousand dollars for the Hollywood film rights, which had a heartening effect upon a man accustomed to thirty-five dollars a week.

During 1935 he tried writing in Mexico but returned to Los Gatos, California. *In Dubious Battle* (1936), concerned with a strike, aroused the critics' fury as Steinbeck had predicted. With a demand for his controversial work, he placed short stories in *Esquire* and *Harper's* and wrote a series of articles for the *San Francisco News* concerning life in California's migrant labor camps, material he used later for *The Grapes of Wrath.*

Of Mice and Men (1937), a popular and a critical success, was selected by the Book-of-the-Month Club, and shortly afterward Steinbeck was selected one of the Ten Outstanding Young Men of the Year. After touring England and Ireland, Russia and Sweden, he produced a play version of the book with the famous playwright, George Kaufman. Steinbeck became a celebrity when the play enjoyed a long run, won the New York Drama Critic Circle's award on the first ballot, and later became a popular film.

Unsurprisingly, however, the night that *Of Mice and Men* opened on Broadway, Steinbeck was living in a migrant camp. In preparation for writing his novels, Steinbeck would often live, work, and be with the people about whom he was to write. Thus, in preparation for writing *The Grapes of Wrath,* Steinbeck went to Oklahoma, joined some migrants and rode with them to California. Once in California, he stayed with the migrants, living with them in "Hoovervilles," joining them in their search for work, and attempting as nearly as possible to come to terms with their essential characteristics. Leaving them, he made several trips to various camps to observe firsthand the living and working conditions of migrants. He wrote some short pieces in which he described the plight of these people, and pleaded for a more tolerant approach in dealing with them. These articles, however, were not very effective. It was only when he molded his new experiences into the form of a novel that positive effects were achieved.

The appearance of *The Grapes of Wrath* was the major publishing event of 1939. *Publishers' Weekly* listed the novel as the best seller of 1939 and the eighth ranking book of 1940. It was estimated that over half a million copies of the original printing were sold. In addition to several American editions, there have been numerous foreign editions and translations. The novel later became one of the important social-protest films. Also in 1940, Steinbeck was elected to membership in the National Institute of Arts and Letters and won the Pulitzer Prize for the best novel of the year as well as the American Bookseller's award.

In 1939 and 1940, Steinbeck set off with Ed Ricketts for expeditions to the Gulf of California, later documented in *The Sea of Cortez.* He also went to Mexico to film *The Forgotten Village,* a semi-documentary about introducing medicine into a suspicious community.

During 1942 his wife sued for divorce and that same year the Army Air Force requested a promotional book, *Bombs Away,* to popularize the flight training program and to allay parental fears about flying. Steinbeck gave the royalties to the Air Forces Aid Society.

Steinbeck's World War II works included the play-novella, *The Moon Is Down,* for which he was decorated by the King of Norway in recognition of the book's contribution to the liberation effort. His film scenario *Lifeboat* is sometimes thought to be his most significant war writing. His human-interest articles, written while he was a special war correspondent for the New York *Herald Tribune* from June to December, 1943, appeared as a collection, *Once There Was a War,* in 1958, Evidently Steinbeck had considered a novel about the war but in *The Wide World of John Steinbeck,* Peter Lisca comments that Steinbeck was "too disheartened by what he had seen of the war to prolong the experience in any way and he decided not to publish it."

Since the war, Steinbeck has devoted himself to novels (*East of Eden*), travels and accounts of his travels, film scripts, and editorials. In 1962, he was awarded the Nobel Prize for literature, the highest honor a writer can receive. Of his many works, *Of Mice and Men* is considered one of his masterpieces.

LIST OF CHARACTERS

George Milton

A farmhand who accepts day labor and who has assumed the responsibility of taking care of his simpleminded friend Lennie.

Lennie Small

A large retarded man who has the mind of a child and who loves to pet soft, pretty things.

Slim

A sympathetic farmhand who understands and consoles George when Lennie is killed

Candy

An old, crippled farmhand who has saved some money and

wants to be a part of George and Lennie's plan to buy a place of their own.

Crooks

A Negro farmhand who keeps to himself and is aloof from the white workers.

Carlson

The farmhand responsible for killing the old, blind dog which belonged to Candy.

Curley

A small, cocky, arrogant man who is the son of the boss.

Curley's Wife

The woman is given no name; she tries to make friends with Lennie.

GENERAL PLOT SUMMARY

George and Lennie have heard that harvesting jobs are available on a nearby farm and are walking there. Instead of hurrying to the farm that night, however, they stop by a stream to camp in the open; they will arrive for work later the next morning. During the evening, George must take a dead mouse away from Lennie, who loves to pet anything soft. George tries to explain to his simpleminded friend that one cannot pet dead things because they are not clean. He reminds Lennie of the trouble he caused when he tried to pet a little girl's dress in the last town.

George knows that Lennie has great difficulty remembering anything; he reminds him many times not to say anything when they go for a job. George also drills Lennie about returning to this particular place if Lennie gets into any trouble. Lennie obediently promises to remember and wants George to tell again about the little place they are going to own someday which will have lots of rabbits for Lennie to take care of.

The next morning, during the job interview, the boss of the farm becomes suspicious when George answers all the questions asked

Lennie. Finally, George must explain that Lennie is not bright, but is a tremendous worker if one only shows him what to do. The boss's son Curley comes into the bunkhouse looking for his wife and asks Lennie some questions. Curley, a small bantam-tempered fellow, likes to pick on people bigger than he is and goads and teases Lennie. After he leaves, Lennie is frightened that something is going to happen and wants to leave this place immediately. George reminds him that the bushes and the stream are safe places to run to in case anything happens.

That night in the bunkhouse, Carlson, one of the farmhands, tells Candy, an old crippled helper, that his dog stinks so badly that they ought to kill it. Candy resists because he has had the dog since it was a pup and doesn't feel right about killing it. After more discussion, Candy is finally coerced into allowing his dog to be killed.

Curley comes into the bunkhouse looking for his wife, and leaves immediately when he hears that Slim, the wagon driver, is down at the barn. The other hands go to the barn to see if there is going to be a fight. After they leave, Lennie wants to hear about the place that he and George are going to own some day and about the rabbits he will tend. George begins the old narrative again; Candy hears it and wants to give them his money if they will let him go along. He knows that soon he will be useless, just like his old dog, which Carlson has just killed. George and Lennie, good-heartedly, decide to accept Candy's offer.

Curley and the other farmhands return from the barn, and when Curley notices that Lennie is grinning, he belligerently begins hitting the bigger man. George finally has to tell Lennie to defend himself; at George's word, Lennie mechanically reaches out and crushes Curley's hand.

On Saturday night, everyone is in town except Lennie, old Candy, and Crooks (the Negro stable keeper). Lennie tells Crooks about the three men's plans, and after the Negro is convinced, he says that he would like to join them and work for nothing. Curley's wife saunters into the shed and is told that she is not wanted. She forces her presence on them, however, and remains until she hears the other men returning from town. Then she slips away.

The next day, Lennie accidentally kills a puppy by playing too hard with it. Curley's wife comes in and tries to talk to him, and after discovering that Lennie likes to feel and pet soft things, she tells him that he can rub her long, soft hair. Lennie, however, strokes it too hard, and when Curley's wife becomes frightened, he holds her so tightly, to keep her from screaming, that he breaks her neck. He now knows that he has done something bad, and knows that he must go back to the hiding place by the stream.

Later Candy comes into the barn and finds the girl's body. He calls George, and they both know instantly that Lennie killed her. George asks Candy to wait a few minutes before he calls the others and George slips into the bunkhouse and steals Carlson's gun. When Curley comes and sees his murdered wife, he is determined to kill Lennie.

George goes straight to the riverside, where he finds Lennie talking to himself. Lennie tries to get George to scold him and, sympathetically, George does so halfheartedly; Lennie asks to be told about the place they are going to get someday, and George then asks Lennie to look across the river and imagine the place they will get. George continues talking about their plans until he hears the others approaching. Then he raises the pistol and shoots Lennie through the back of the head. Curley and the others arrive and congratulate George for killing Lennie.

Summaries and Commentaries

CHAPTER ONE

Summary

Two men are walking along a hot, dusty road and stop by a stream for a drink of water. Lennie, the larger of the men, drinks deeply from the stream, although George warns him to be careful because the water might not be safe. After George drinks a small amount, they sit down to rest. Lennie wonders where they are going and George is disgusted that Lennie has already forgotten. He explains again that they are going to work on a farm not too far away and that Lennie is not to say anything when they reach the farmhouse.

George notices that Lennie is hiding something in his pocket, and he forces the bigger man to hand it over. It is a dead mouse that Lennie found alongside the road and has been petting. George takes the mouse and hurls it away. He reminds Lennie that petting things has always gotten them in trouble, especially in the last town; Lennie, however, has already forgotten the episode. George sends Lennie after some sticks in order to make a fire and promises to let him have a match to light the fire. When Lennie comes back wet and with only one stick, George knows that Lennie has retrieved the dead mouse. He takes it away again, trying to explain that this mouse is not fresh and is not good for petting.

After Lennie collects enough wood, George takes out three cans of beans to warm up for their supper. Lennie wishes that he had some ketchup to go on his, and George reminds him that they don't have any. George suddenly explodes with anger, explaining all the things he could do if he weren't tied down with Lennie. After George complains some more, Lennie volunteers to go away and live in a cave somewhere by himself. Then George feels sorry for being so mean and, at Lennie's request, he begins to tell about their plans to buy a little farm all their own where Lennie can raise rabbits and just the two of them will live there "off the fatta the lan'."

George decides to spend the night here by the stream and show up the next day for work. Before going to sleep, he tells Lennie to remember this place because if Lennie ever gets into trouble he must return here and hide in the bushes. Lennie promises to try to remember, but his mind is thinking more about the rabbits that they are going to have someday.

Commentary

The dominant contrast in the first part of the chapter is between the enormous physical strength of Lennie and the small, restless, sharp features of George. Even though George is the smaller, he has to look after his clumsy, retarded companion. The two men are, in every sense of the word, diametrically opposite. At the same time, however, the reader should be aware of the bond that exists between George and Lennie, especially when other men demonstrate such an intense personal loneliness. Therefore, even though George seems rough and harsh toward Lennie, the sensitive reader should note George's strong current of attachment to his simpleminded companion.

Furthermore, toward the end of the chapter when George is supposedly angry at Lennie, he recounts all the things he could do if he didn't have to look after Lennie. He says that he could "stay in a cat house all night" and could drink a gallon of whiskey the first of every month and play as much pool as he wants to. Furthermore, George thinks that he would be able to get and keep a job if he didn't have to take care of Lennie. However, the point is later made that all the people who work on the various farms and ranches are free to go into town and do all these things. Yet they are miserable, since they do these things only because they don't have anyone else. But Lennie and George do have each other and that means a lot to this type of nomadic person.

The opening descriptions of the novel emphasize the cooling and healing effects of the country stream. Later we hear that George and Lennie had to hide in an irrigation ditch in water up to their necks in order to escape the men who were looking for them; but here, the water seems to imply a quality of peace and safety. This opening description also introduces the motif of the rabbits. As George and Lennie arrive, the rabbits, which were occupying the place by the stream, "hurried noiselessly for cover." Lennie will be identified with rabbits throughout the novel and his dream of happiness involves having as many rabbits as possible to pet, play with, and tend to. Also, he is often described as moving as noiselessly as a rabbit in spite of his huge, lumbering physique. Likewise, when Lennie drinks from the stream, the description of his actions suggests an animal drinking.

Part of Lennie's charm lies in the perfectly innocent and childlike joys he participates in. We have descriptions of his happily playing with one finger in the water and wanting George to join him in his simple pleasures. There is an innocence underscoring his every act in spite of how society might interpret them, and his life never rises above the simplest acts and pleasures. His devotion to petting small animals is an indication of his basic simplicity. To Lennie, it does not matter if the animal is dead; he accepts it almost as readily as he would a live one, disclosing how completely he functions outside the realm of normal distinctions.

Lennie, therefore, is like an animal in that he devotes himself to the basic responses to life and, like a pet dog, he has a complete and utter devotion to George. When George sits by the bank of the river, Lennie tries to imitate George's exact manner and position. Later, when George makes Lennie give up the mouse, Lennie is described in terms of a terrier who must obey his master even though he does not want to. Lennie's love of little things contrasts well with his big build and suggests that his mind functions like a little child's rather than like his big brawny body. But ironically it is his big body which secures jobs for them. He is able to do the work of several men on any given day.

George's manner of talking to Lennie should be contrasted with the strong protective feelings he has about Lennie. Dealing with the mind that Lennie possesses, George must be a strong disciplinarian who drills, forcefully, things into Lennie's mind. We should also be aware of George's oft-repeated statement that he does not do things just to be cruel; instead, he is acting for Lennie's own good. This should be kept constantly before the reader's mind so that every act that George commits can be seen as performed for Lennie's good, especially in the final chapters when George has to kill his companion.

Along this same line, we can understand George's annoyance when Lennie forgets things so easily. We find out later in the chapter that, when excited, Lennie cannot remember anything. This forgetting is the flaw which caused much of their trouble in the past. Combined with Lennie's instinctive and innocent desire to touch pretty things, his strength and his forgetfulness caused him to hold on to a little girl in the last town until she screamed for help. Thus George and Lennie both had to hide from the posse of men wanting to hang Lennie. Furthermore, George wants Lennie to remember certain things so that he will never get into trouble again. At the end of this chapter, we hear George wants Lennie to remember where this particular hiding place is in case Lennie gets into trouble. It is almost incredible that Lennie does actually remember this place after he murders Curley's wife. Essentially then, George continually demonstrates a rough but highly protective nature toward his retarded companion.

The question is raised in this chapter as to whether a person is guilty of a crime if he can't remember or does not know that it is a crime. Lennie can't remember why they had to leave the last town and the job in that town. He can't even remember that they were chased out of the town. The only image that is clear to him is the vision of a future life where there will be lots of little rabbits for him to tend.

The scene in which George is griping about how Lennie caused them to get run out of town provides some basic exposition and gives us an analogy to a future event. Steinbeck is masterful here in the casual and seemingly insignificant way that he lets the reader know that Lennie is attracted to pretty things and that Lennie had tried to feel a young girl's dress because it was bright and pretty. Of equal importance is the fact that this past event will foreshadow the death of Curley's wife when Lennie tries to pet her pretty hair.

It is an ironic indication of the quality of Lennie's mind that after George has finished with his bitter outburst, Lennie thinks it was all caused by his desire for some ketchup for his beans. He only senses that George is angry and, therefore, returns to his most recent offense—asking for ketchup.

The place where Lennie and George spend the night suggests a certain contentment and peace in life. This will, in one sense, be their last place together. It prompts Lennie to ask George to describe, once again, their future place. Lennie has heard the dream so many times that he can recite it as well as George, but as with children, Lennie takes delight in hearing a familiar story being retold.

As George narrates the story about the place they plan to buy one day, we become aware that even these people—the lowest on the social ladder—still have their ideals and dreams. Furthermore, we realize that earlier when George was wishing that he did not have to look after Lennie, George was only lying. Now he says that "Guys like us, that work on ranches, are the loneliest guys in the world. They got no fambly. They don't belong no place." But he continues to explain that "with us it ain't like that. We got a future. We got somebody to talk to that gives a damn about us." Thus, involved in the dream of a place of their own, is the fact that they have each other while the other people of the world who go to the "cat house" and play pool and drink a "gallon of liquor" are the really lonely people of the world.

This dream will become more significant as we see that other hired hands have had the same dream and want to participate in George and Lennie's plans. In other words, the tragedy of George and Lennie is not just one isolated and pathetic event, but is more representative than we would at first assume.

Toward the end of the chapter, George promises Lennie that someday he will get a pup for him to pet. In a very short time, Lennie will get a pup but will pet it so hard that he kills it—an act which will foreshadow and magnify the murder of Curley's wife.

Finally, it is noteworthy, that the chapter ends *not* with George's ominous warning that Lennie come back to this place if he gets in trouble; *instead,* the chapter ends with Lennie's dream about the rabbits. This dream is, as is the entire novel, narrated in a style that is so seemingly simple and direct as to suggest that there was no especial skill used in writing. But a close examination reveals that Steinbeck has devoted much care to polishing and creating a construction of parallels and rhythms. This at-first-glance simplicity in his style blends readily with the deceptive depth of his subject matter.

CHAPTER TWO

Summary

George and Lennie arrive at the farm about ten in the morning and hear that the boss was expecting them the preceding day. When George examines his bunk, he discovers a can of insect powder and is angry because of the implications. He is told that the place is very clean and that the can belonged to a man who had quit some days ago. He also hears that the boss is a "pretty nice fella," and in a few minutes, the boss appears. George has to explain that the bus driver did not let them off at the right place and they had to walk too far to make it in one day.

When the boss asks for the names of the two men, George answers for Lennie and ultimately has to explain the Lennie is not "real bright" but assures the boss that Lennie is a powerful worker. When the boss becomes suspicious that George is taking advantage of Lennie, George explains that they are cousins and that he has been looking after Lennie for a long time. The boss is finally pacified and leaves.

After George talks a bit more to Lennie about being careful, he finds that an old man has been listening outside. The old man, Candy, is crippled, tends to the small chores around the ranch, and is accompanied by an old lame sheepdog with "pale, blind old eyes." While Candy is explaining that he wasn't listening, Curley, the boss's son comes in looking for his old man. He sees Lennie staring at him and begins to ask Lennie some questions. George answers for him even though Curley is talking directly to Lennie. Curley is antagonistic and orders Lennie to answer in the future when he is spoken to.

After Curley leaves, Candy explains that Curley was once a light-weight boxer and always likes to start fights with people bigger than he is. George notices that Curley looks like a "mean little guy," and Candy explains that he is worse now than usual because he has just married a "tart" who is giving him trouble. When Lennie and George are alone, George once again reminds Lennie that if there is trouble that he must go back to the bush by the river and hide.

While they are talking, Curley's wife appears, looking for her husband; she stands in the doorway long after she hears that Curley has gone. Lennie stares at her, and afterward when George reprimands him for staring, Lennie wants to leave this place at once. "This ain't no good place," he says. "Le's get outa here. It's mean here." But George tells him that they must stay and get a stake so they can buy a farm.

Slim, one of the farmhands, comes in for lunch, and after meeting George and Lennie, hopes that they will be on his working team. Carlson, another farmhand, comes in and hears that Slim's dog had a litter of puppies the night before. They talk about giving old Candy one in place of the old blind mutt he has now. Slim explains that he had to drown four of the puppies because his bitch couldn't feed them all. After they leave, Lennie wants George to ask for one of the puppies for him, and George promises to do so. Curley comes by again looking for his wife, and George tells him that she is out looking for him. George is afraid that he is going to tangle with Curley.

Commentary

In this novel, Steinbeck is developing carefully and slowly a situation where his characters can be seen to interact against each other and against a certain situation. He is concerned with character development and creating a mood such as the ominous feeling connected with Curley's visits in this chapter. That is, without being able to identify it exactly, we can say that Curley evokes an indefinite feeling of fear and foreboding.

The bunkhouse with its bare, sparse furnishings contrasts to the dream that George and Lennie have of a place of their own. It even offers a contrast to the peace and quiet of their bed by the stream in the last chapter. This is emphasized ironically when George finds the can of powder for lice and loudly objects to living in a place with "pants rabbits"—the name commonly given to lice.

Candy, the old lame worker who shows them around, will be more fully developed as one of the lonely people who don't belong to anything. He will later try to join Lennie and George in their dream of owning their own place. His only companion now is the old blind and lame dog which he has had since it was a pup.

This chapter makes it clear why George wanted to spend the night at the river and arrive at work during the morning. If he had come at night, there would have been too many people for Lennie to meet and George was afraid that Lennie would have become confused and would have ruined their chances of getting the jobs. But while the other people are off working, George can cover for Lennie better, since they have only to contend with one person at a time. Thus, in the first interview with the boss, George has to do all the answering for Lennie. He does not try to disguise the fact that Lennie is somewhat retarded but strongly emphasizes Lennie's working ability. The natural assumption of the boss is that George is taking advantage of Lennie and will probably steal his wages. This is ironic because, to be brutal, Lennie is more trouble than his wages are worth; but to assure the boss that there is no dishonesty involved, George claims Lennie as a cousin.

Before the interview with the boss, George had warned Lennie not to say anything, but while they were talking, Lennie forgot again and repeated George's statement "strong as a bull." He is immediately ashamed of having forgotten, but it is too late. In essence, this is a small and insignificant event, but when we apply it to the total work, we see that Steinbeck is weaving even into his small details the greater theme of Lennie's forgetfulness, which will later cause him to kill the little pup and, climactically, Curley's wife.

As noted above, the appearance of Curley brings an ominous note into the novel. George's immediate response to him was that he does not like a mean little guy; significantly, the one thing that the huge Lennie does not want to do is to hurt someone. If he does so, as with the rabbits or the mice or the pup, it is entirely accidental. In contrast the small Curley delights in hurting people, especially if they are larger than he is. Thus we have the contrast, not just in the physical size of the two men, but also in the fact that the big man does not want to hurt things and accidentally destroys small things, while the small man delights in trying to hurt larger people.

Candy sees through Curley's essential nature when he says: "Never did seem right to me"; then explaining that Curley will attack a big guy and if he wins, then he is a game little fighter, but if he gets beaten "then ever'body says the big guy oughta pick somebody his own size." He concludes that "Curley ain't givin' nobody a chance." In a sense this is what will happen to Lennie— no one will give him a chance.

George's reaction to Curley is also revealing. If in the end of the novel, we understand George's killing Lennie, then we need to know some of his basic beliefs and views. In the preceding chapter, we saw how deeply committed George was to the protection of Lennie and that he would never intentionally do anything mean to him. Other than this, however, what type of ethics does George possess? In this chapter, we find that George disapproves of the fact that Curley talks about his private relationships with his wife. Concerning the glove full of vaseline, he says "That's a dirty thing to tell around." Thus, we can basically say that George is not just the average shiftless man but one who is aware of many facets of life and who has a strong sense of right and wrong, intensified by his care of Lennie.

When George and Lennie are alone, George expresses his fear of what might happen. Like old Candy, he knows that Curley is a type who is going to try to hit Lennie merely because Lennie is such a big man. It is an ironic contrast of events that Lennie is also frightened and pleads with little Goerge to protect him from the little Curley. These fears cause George to once more drill into Lennie's memory the hideout place—the bushes by the stream—in case there is trouble. George wants to prepare for the worst, and Lennie cannot be concerned about the trouble, except that then he would not be allowed to tend the rabbits.

The sense of fear that George feels is intensified as soon as Curley's wife appears and hangs around the bunkhouse. The wife is obviously dressed like a loose woman and conducts herself in a common, vulgar manner. To the simpleminded Lennie, she is a very beautiful person, and he cannot help staring at her as he would stare at anything that he found pretty. Lennie's complete innocence is echoed in his remark that he thought the wife very "purty." However much sexual implication is indicated by these looks must be interpreted by the individual reader. Essentially, Steinbeck does not eliminate the possibility that Lennie is sexually attracted to her, but he does not make this the central point of their first meeting.

George immediately perceives that the wife is "a tramp." Of course, George and Lennie are also tramps, but in an entirely different use of the term. Furthermore, George knows that she should not have been in the bunkhouse, and her presence is the cause of additional fears. It is also significant that after her departure, Lennie for the first time is frightened. Earlier, he had cried out that he did not want Curley to hit him, but this was a specific case of physical encounter. Now Lennie feels a more abstract and indefinite fear, but he can only say: "This ain't no good place. . . . Le's get outa here. It's mean here." It is as though Lennie has the instinctive knowledge and fear of a child and can intuit that something bad will happen in this place.

George explains to Lennie that they can't leave because they have to stay in order to get a stake. He is thinking of the need to get some money ahead so that they can buy their own little place. Thus they must endure this present hardship in order to fulfill their dream, but ironically, this situation will be the total destruction of their dream and ultimately it would have been better if they had pulled up and left.

Slim, the jerkline skinner, comes in and is seen to be a person who commands respect and who invites confidence. His character will become important later, because he will be the one who will assure George that killing Lennie is necessary. Slim also admires the fact that George and Lennie travel together, but finds it unusual that two people have managed to stay together. Also, Slim owns the bitch dog which has just had a litter of puppies. Again, we meet the motif of birth and death here because as this dog has just had puppies, we hear of the killing of Candy's old dog. Also Lennie will receive one of the puppies and will, through love, kill it.

Lennie, who is usually oblivious to things around him, has heard Slim tell about the puppies and has also heard that Slim had to kill four of the litter because the mother could not feed them all. Notice that Lennie does not have to ask George to get him one because George knows automatically that Lennie wants one and promises to get him one. Gradually, then, even in small items the life-death motif is emerging and preparing the way for the final catastrophe of the novel, especially since the chapter ends with an emphasis on the old dog who will soon be killed.

Before the chapter ends, however, Curley makes one more appearance looking for his wife. This offers further indications of the mounting frustration working in Curley and warns the reader that he will be a troublemaker.

Steinbeck's technique of writing has often been referred to as cinematic, that is, as being so objective that it is as though we were watching a motion picture. This chapter illustrates that technique rather clearly. It is filled with short scenes, each contributing some-thing to the total development, and each scene is narrated as though we were looking into the bunkhouse and observing the actual action ourselves. While Lennie and George are in the bunkhouse, there appear Candy, the boss, Curley, Curley's wife, Slim, and Carlson. Each time, the scene is simply narrated without any intrusion from the author. The objectivity of Steinbeck's narration can be seen by comparing this chapter with his dramatic version, which utilizes most of the conversation.

CHAPTER THREE

Summary

In the evening, George thanks Slim for giving Lennie one of the puppies. Slim was glad to do it because he would probably have killed them anyway. He comments about what a good worker Lennie is and still finds it unusual that the two of them travel around together. George explains that they were born in the same town and after Lennie's aunt died, he just followed George around and now they are used to each other. George tells how he used to play jokes on Lennie, but Lennie never understood it was a joke and so there was no fun in it. He explains about the trouble Lennie got into at the last town, but asserts that Lennie is not cruel. Slim agrees that Lennie "ain't a bit mean."

In a few minutes, Lennie comes in walking, hunched over. George knows immediately that Lennie has one of the puppies with him and he makes him take it back to the barn, warning Lennie that he could easily kill the puppy by handling it too much. Lennie silently obeys George, and Slim notes that Lennie is exactly like a child.

Carlson comes in and complains that Candy's old dog stinks. He wants Candy to kill the dog, but Candy can't do it because they have been together since the dog was a pup. Carlson gets Slim to promise him another of the young puppies and then Carlson promises to shoot the dog for Candy. He explains that the dog is so old and crippled that to put it out of its misery would be the humane thing to do. Candy still cannot agree and Carlson says that the stench is so bad that they can't sleep. After more badgering, Candy finally agrees to let the dog be killed.

After Carlson leaves, there is silence in the room as everyone waits to hear the gunshot. Whit, another farmhand, tells George about a house of prostitution in the town where they can sit and enjoy themselves, and George agrees to go along, but he is not going to spend money on one of the women because he and Lennie have to get a stake together.

Curley comes in looking for his wife and is told that she in not in the bunkhouse. He wants to know where Slim is and is told that Slim went to the barn. Curley flies out the door toward the barn and some of the men follow to see if Curley and Slim will tangle. After they leave, Lennie asks George to tell about the place they are going to get. George begins again to tell how the place has an orchard and a little house and other things. It is a place where they will belong and no one can run them off.

Old Candy has overheard the conversation and he asks about the place and wonders if he could join them because he has about three hundred dollars saved up. He explains that pretty soon he will be treated in the same way as his dog was and he would like to live on a place where he belonged. George decides to accept Candy's offer and it is almost certain that in a month they will be able to buy the place.

Curley and Slim come back and they are arguing about Curley's wife. Lennie is still smiling about the dream. Curley notices Lennie's smile and thinks that he is laughing at him. He immediately begins hitting Lennie, who makes no effort to protect himself until George yells at him to get Curley. Lennie reaches out and very easily crushes Curley's hand. Slim forces Curley to concur that his hand was hurt in a machine and that no one will be fired. Curley agrees and after they take him to the hospital, Lennie wonders if he will still be able to tend the rabbits on the new place.

Commentary

The character of Slim is further developed in this chapter. He is glad to give Lennie one of the puppies and he recognizes the unusual value of the relationship between George and Lennie. He knows that Lennie is not a mean person and can, therefore, sympathize more acutely with George's later position when George must kill Lennie. In fact, this chapter emphasizes rather strongly again that Lennie is, by nature, just a simple little child without a mean impulse. Thus, whatever he does is not committed out of cruelty but out of his simpleminded way of understanding things. Furthermore, as illustrated by the episode where George told Lennie to jump in the river for a joke, Lennie cannot even remember long enough to bear a grudge. When George pulled him out of the river, Lennie was grateful for George's help and had completely forgotten it was George who had told him to jump in in the first place.

While Slim and George are talking, Lennie comes in trying to hide something. George knows immediately that Lennie has brought the puppy with him and he must make Lennie take it back to the barn. Lennie's act simply shows his strong devotion and need for something to love. Furthermore, the manner in which George has to discipline Lennie again emphasizes Lennie's childlike qualities. As Slim says, "He's jus' like a kid, ain't he?"

The central event in this chapter is the death of old Candy's dog. There are many parallels between Candy and his old dog and George and Lennie. The dog is old and basically a nuisance because it stinks so badly. Candy insists though that he has been with the dog so long that he doesn't notice the stench. Lennie is at times a nuisance to George because Lennie is constantly getting into trouble, but as George says, he has been with Lennie so long now that they are used to each other. Thus, each gains a sense of belonging simply by having either the dog, as with Candy, or by having Lennie, as with George. When the dog is destroyed, notice that Candy will then search for some other way to belong. It would be difficult, however, to predict the same for George.

Carlson is not being base and evil when he suggests that the old dog should be shot. It is one of those necessary things in life. Even the more sensitive and sympathetic Slim agrees that the dog should be shot in the same way that at the end he tells George that it is necessary to kill Lennie, but unlike George, Candy cannot perform the actual act of killing. After the act is completed he admits to George that he should have shot the dog himself.

Steinbeck divides the scene into two sections. Before Candy gives his assent for the death of the dog, there is an interlude in which they discuss a letter in a western magazine. This interlude gives Candy time to think about the proposition, so that when Carlson returns to the subject, Candy will agree. When Candy does so, notice that he cannot look at the dog, but just turns his face to the wall. It will virtually be the same with George in the last chapter. He will make Lennie look the other way before he is able to pull the trigger.

The motif of life-death is thus restated in two terms. Lennie keeps bringing the puppy into the bunkhouse or taking the puppy away from its mother. This could cause the pup to die. Then, there is the actual death of the old dog. While the men are waiting for the shot which will announce the death of Candy's dog, an unusual silence pervades the bunkhouse. The men are highly conscious of and sensitive to the dog's death. They realize that the dog had meant a lot to old Candy. This reaction should be kept in mind when we come to the end of the novel, because then only Slim will be sympathetic to the death of Lennie. Ultimately then there seems to be more sympathy for the death of the old dog than there will be for the death of Lennie. Notice also that after the shot is heard, Slim and the others attempt feebly either to get away or to make some kind of conversation in order not to think about the event.

We hear some more reports about Curley's wife which indicate that she is willing to talk to anyone at any time. This foreshadows her attempt to talk to Lennie in chapter five. George is also told about the house of prostitution in the town where the men can get a decent drink and relax for a time. George is going to accompany the men, but he refuses to spend the money for a prostitute because he and Lennie have to get a stake together. Thus, returning to the first chapter, we can now say that Lennie's friendship and the dream of owning a place is much more important than the good times that George is always complaining about missing.

When the farmhands follow Curley to the barn to watch the encounter with Slim, Lennie asks George to tell about the place they are going to get. George tells again about all the things they can expect as soon as they get their stake together. The repetition of the dream serves to emphasize the difference between George and Lennie and the typical farmhand. The fact that they belong to each other and that they are actually working at fulfilling their dream sets them apart from the others.

It is important to the theme of the novel that Candy has been listening to George tell about the dream and wants to participate in it. Note also that when Candy asks about the farm George becomes defensive. He knows that such dreams are open to ridicule because so few people have the ability or the drive to fulfill them. Candy's desire to belong is even more significant, since he has just lost his dog. He feels that he too is old, like the dog, and that what happened to his dog is about to happen to him. Thus, he needs desperately a place to which he can belong. As Candy says: "You seen what they done to my dog tonight? They says he wasn't no good to himself nor nobody else. When they can me here I wisht somebody'd shoot me." But Candy knows that they won't and that he will have to go to a county home.

Nor is it just that Candy needs a place to belong; after the loss of his dog, he also needs comradeship. Man cannot live alone, and the relationship between George and Lennie assumes more importance now. Ultimately this idea should be held in mind because it makes the act of killing Lennie more important, for it leaves George in a worse situation than he has ever been in.

Candy's desire to join the group serves another function. Since he has almost three hundred dollars saved up, his money makes the dream *almost* a reality. As in many classical dreams, the middle portions offer a hope of the dream coming true. Here this nearness to fulfillment makes the final catastrophe even more tragic.

After Candy is accepted by George and Lennie, he admits to George that he should have been the one to have shot his own dog. This might be applied to George's final action. He, and he alone, is the only person to kill Lennie. It would be extremely cruel to allow Lennie to be trapped like an animal by the other men.

The end of the chapter offers one more threat of disaster as Curley intentionally starts a fight with Lennie. Note that Lennie's only offense was that he was still smiling with delight over the prospects of having his own place. Curley thinks that the big man is laughing at him. Lennie does not use his strength until George tells him to and then Curley is like a piece of paper in Lennie's hands. He crushes Curley's hand with no visible effort. This feat of strength prepares us to accept readily how easy it will be for Lennie to accidentally kill Curley's wife, and this scene prepares us for the strong desire for revenge against Lennie that Curley will demonstrate. Lennie's only concern about the fight and Curley's maimed hand is whether or not he will be allowed to tend to the rabbits.

CHAPTER FOUR

Summary

Crooks was the Negro stable buck who lived alone in a shed of the barn. He was a proud man who kept aloof from the other farm-hands, and demanded that they keep their distance from him. On Saturday night, he was sitting alone when Lennie, smiling simple-mindedly, appeared at the doorway. Crooks told him that this room was private. Lennie doesn't understand even when Crooks explains a black man does not associate with a white man. Crooks tells Lennie to go look at the puppies, and "don't come in a place where you're not wanted." Woodenly, Lennie stands there looking confused until Crooks finally allows him to come into the room.

Once inside, Lennie begins to talk about the rabbits he is going to raise and be nice to when he and George get their farm. Crooks becomes sarcastic and ridicules the plan as just another wild dream. He even begins to tease Lennie about George disappearing and never coming back. This suggestion confuses Lennie; he insists, pleadingly, that George would not leave him. Then, as Lennie is about to become enraged, Crooks explains that he was only "supposing."

Crooks cannot believe that George and Lennie are actually going to get some land. He has heard, so often, so many drifting farm-workers planning to get their own little piece of land; no one, however, has ever done so. Candy comes looking for Lennie to explain some more of his "figuring" about what they can do on the farm. Crooks is still doubtful that they will actually get the farm, but he listens more intently. He begins to lose some of his doubts when he hears that they have already saved up almost enough money to get some land. Then, he tells them how lonesome he gets and how he would like to work for them just for his keep.

Curley's wife appears at the door looking for her husband. The men tell her that her husband is not around and suggest that she return to the house. Curley's wife doesn't leave, however, and because she too is lonely, stays and asks more questions. She remembers out loud how once some man offered to put her "in pitchers"; now she has to hang around the barn talking to "a nigger an' a dum-dum, and a lousy ol' sheep." Candy has heard enough and tries to make her leave them alone. She refuses and turns her attention to Lennie, who only becomes confused. Crooks then orders her out of his room, and she turns viciously on him threatening him and reminding him what a white woman could do to a Negro if she wanted to. Crooks, defeatedly, resumes his seat. She then turns on Candy and threatens him. Lennie anxiously wishes that George would come back, and at that moment, Candy hears the wagons coming through the farm gate. Curley's wife slips out before her husband gets there.

When George finds Lennie and Candy in Crooks' room, he orders them out. He is also annoyed that Candy has been telling someone else about their plans. As they are leaving, Crooks calls out to Candy to forget about including him in their plans—he doesn't want to go to such a place anyway. After they leave, Crooks resumes his lonely existence.

Commentary

With the beginning of chapter four, we start the second half of the story and meet a new character—Crooks, "the Negro stable buck." Crooks has been mentioned earlier, but now we see him as the axis of a scene. He is described as a "proud, aloof man. He kept his distance and demanded that other people keep theirs." This description, however, fits Crooks only in terms of his outward characteristics. Actually, he is aware of the arbitrary social distinctions which are created as a result of his being Negro, and the distance he maintains is one generated by his refusal to accept a subservient position. Since he knows that he is not accepted by the white people, he then assumes the role of a distant and self-contained person.

No one has ever tried to visit Crooks' quarters because the white farmhands are aware of social prejudice and distinction. Lennie, however, in his simple ways, only sees Crooks as another human being and makes no direct social distinctions. It would seem that Steinbeck is implying that such artificial social distrinctions are the product of cultivated prejudice. Lennie's complete acceptance of Crooks must be contrasted with Curley's wife's treatment of Crooks later in the chapter. Whereas Lennie accepts Crooks with perfect naturalness, Curley's wife uses the color line to threaten Crooks.

She reminds him what would happen to a Negro man if a white woman were to complain about him, particularly if the white woman suggested that the Negro were guilty of sexual advances.

Crooks has been alone so long that he does not know how to receive Lennie at first. He tells Lennie not to come where he is not wanted, and it is only gradually that he allows Lennie to enter his room. Crooks then begins defensively to taunt Lennie so cruelly that Lennie becomes confused. Crooks is apparently taking out all of his repressions on this simpleminded white person and is making Lennie the scapegoat for all of his rejections by the whites. Ultimately, Crooks is trying to make Lennie feel what it is like not to have anyone to talk to. "A guy needs somebody—to be near him." Thus, this chapter re-emphasizes the need for friendship and comradeship introduced through the close association of Lennie and George. Furthermore, Lennie's determination that George will come back emphasizes that, without George, Lennie is absolutely helpless; thus, at the end of the story, George knows this and the only course open to him is to kill Lennie. This theme of loneliness introduced by Crooks foreshadows George's situation because soon he will be without comradeship, after he kills Lennie.

Crooks refuses to believe in the dream that Lennie has of owning his own place because he has seen too many drifters who have talked about owning a little piece of land and who never accomplished their dream. After Candy comes in and tells Crooks that they already have the money, Crooks questioningly reverses his opinion and wonders if he can join them. He would be willing to work for nothing. This offer emphasizes the dire loneliness of the man and his need to "belong." By contrast, we can assume that the relationship between George and Lennie is indeed a rare one.

This loneliness theme is given depth by the appearance of Curley's wife; she is also lonely and comes so often to the barn because there is no one to talk to and, like Crooks, she feels so alien. The extent of her loneliness is expressed by her acknowledgment of her basic dislike for her husband and her willingness to talk to a "bunch of bindle stiffs—a nigger an' a dum-dum and a lousy ol' sheep." Furthermore, Curley's wife has her own dream which revolves about her past chances for becoming an actress in the movies. Her explanation of her dream contrasts to the dream of land that the three were talking about before her entry. Each, then, is reminded of his personal dream and Candy tries to get rid of Curley's wife because he sees her as a direct threat to their dream. Ironically, she will be the instrument of destruction to the dream, but a passive instrument, since she has no overt designs to destroy their ideals.

Notice that not only does Candy try to force her to leave, but Crooks begins to defend his newfound friends and orders Curley's wife to leave. Curley's wife, however, is not intimidated by three such people and threatens to destroy them all. It turns out that she is the strongest, and Crooks and old Candy have to retreat into their protective shells. Crooks, particularly, is defeated and sees that if he does enter into a white world, even for a minute, he is thrown into confusion. At the end, then, he retracts his earlier offer to work for nothing, knowing now that the dream could never be realized.

CHAPTER FIVE

Summary

On Sunday afternoon, most of the farmhands are playing horseshoes, but Lennie has been playing with his puppy and has played too rough and killed it. He is afraid now that George won't let him tend the rabbits, but vaguely feels that this wasn't "No bad thing like I got to go hide in the brush." He thinks of burying the puppy and not letting anyone know, but he then realizes that George would, somehow, automatically (like God) know.

While Lennie is trying to decide what to do, Curley's wife comes into the barn. Lennie won't talk to her because George told him that he couldn't tend the rabbits if he did. Curley's wife can't understand this and tries to explain how lonely she gets. She then notices that Lennie has something covered up and discovers that it is just the dead puppy. She assures Lennie that it was just a mutt and that no one will be upset over its death.

Even though Lennie tells her over and over that he is not supposed to talk with her, Curley's wife does not leave. She even begins to tell Lennie secret things. She reveals that she doesn't even like her husband. Lennie can think only of whether or not he will be allowed to tend the rabbits when George finds out about the puppy. Curley's wife wants to know why Lennie is so attached to rabbits. Lennie laboriously tries to explain how he likes to pet nice things. Once he even had a piece of velvet, which he stroked until he lost it.

Curley's wife thinks that Lennie is nuts but she still understands vaguely what he means. She explains that she likes to stroke her own hair when she is combing it. She offers to let Lennie feel how soft it is. He begins to stroke it and when he "pets" too hard, she cries for him to quit and tries to jerk away. Lennie becomes frightened and holds on to her. She tries to scream and Lennie covers her mouth because George would be so mad if he discovered them together. As she struggles to free herself, Lennie pleads with her not to cause him any trouble because then he would not get to tend the rabbits. He shakes her a little bit, and when he quits, she is limp and silent. Suddenly Lennie realizes that he has done a bad thing and that he will have to go hide in the brush.

He picks up the dead puppy, hides it under his coat and slips out of the barn. Later, Candy comes into the barn looking for Lennie. He sees Curley's wife lying limp and silent. He tries to awaken her and then realizes that she is dead. He goes immediately to find George.

As soon as George sees the body, he knows that Lennie killed her. Candy wonders if this is the end of their plans to get a little place. George says he will stay and work out his month and then will go to "some lousy cat house" and spend all his money. George asks Candy to stay there for a minute and then call the other hired hands so that he will have time to go into the bunkhouse.

After George leaves, Candy futilely curses Curley's wife for causing all the trouble. He then goes after the other farmhands. Curley sees his wife's body and intuitively knows that Lennie has killed her; he is determined to get revenge. He orders the other men to get guns and join him. George tries to get Curley not to shoot Lennie, but Curley is determined to kill him. Carlson comes in and reports that Lennie has stolen his pistol. Curley orders George to stick close to them, and they leave with the men to track down and kill Lennie.

Commentary

Lennie is seen playing with his puppy and we discover that he has just killed it. This first killing prepares the reader for the death of Curley's wife later on because now we know that Lennie can't remember, and we realize how fervently he desires to pet soft things even though he does not understand how to be gentle. Lennie does know that this killing of the puppy is not serious enough for him to go hide where George told him to, but he also fears his action might be so offensive that George will not let him tend the rabbits.

While Lennie is emotionally struggling over the death of the puppy, Curley's wife appears. She too is lonely and disturbed; consequently, even though Lennie does remember that he is not to talk with her, their mutual problems lead them into some type of communication. When she sympathizes with him about the puppy and assures him that no one will care, Lennie feels consoled and appreciative toward this woman, who then tells him about her own dream. She even confesses to Lennie that she can't stand her husband. The irony is that as she tells about her dream of leaving Curley and becoming an actress, her narration will lead to her death and to the destruction of Lennie's dream of having a place and living "offa th' fat of th' lan'."

The communication between the two people, then, is a result of the basic loneliness of Curley's wife and the basic desire for consolation in Lennie. This desire leads to more direct confidences from Curley's wife. It is also ironic when we see how much she dislikes her husband because in a short time, he will want to kill Lennie to avenge her death.

The confidential manner in which Curley's wife talks to Lennie allows him to confess why he likes soft things. Curley's wife pretends to understand and when she offers to let Lennie feel the softness of her hair, we immediately remember the many times Lennie has killed something soft because he wants to pet it too hard. Thus, when he strokes the woman's hair, we see the pattern climactically repeated; she becomes frightened at his hard manner of petting and struggles futilely to free herself.

We now can return to the first chapter of the novel and recall that when someone gets frightened in Lennie's presence, he freezes and holds even more tightly to the object. Furthermore, the dream of the rabbits is about to be realized and he knows if he makes one more mistake that he will not be allowed to tend the bunnies. He has also just killed the puppy and has, in addition, violated George's command that he not talk to Curley's wife. All these fast-building factors combine to paralyze Lennie's strength and cause him to hold even faster to anything—anything stable in this crumbling emotional world of his.

The emphasis throughout this scene is not upon the dying woman, but instead, upon Lennie's fright and terror. We feel only in a peripheral sense the struggling of the woman; instead, we see the pathetic fear of Lennie as he begins to whimper and cry and beg the woman not to scream because if she does he will not get to tend the rabbits. Furthermore, he keeps emphasizing that she is going to get him in trouble "jus' like George said." As Lennie's mind becomes more shaken about the trouble he might get in, he begins to shake the woman, and jerking her spasmodically, he snaps her neck. With this crack, the dream shatters and is forever destroyed. Again, the reader should review the scene to observe the masterful way in which Steinbeck has kept the attention focused on Lennie's problem; the woman functions only as an abstract obstacle which is confronting Lennie with potential trouble. If Steinbeck had focused on the victim of the murder, the reader's sympathy would not have been with the simpleminded Lennie; that is, the reader would have been horrified by the crime rather than feeling compassion for the retarded mind which precipitated the deed.

As with the puppy, Lennie once again knows that he has "done wrong," and knows also that this is a "real bad thing" which will necessitate his going to hide in the brush. The irony is that he can remember the brush where he was supposed to hide, but could not remember other things that George told him. The rationalization for this is simply that Lennie becomes easily confused in the presence of others, but alone, and like an animal, can instinctively sense that he should go hide. Before leaving, he tries to cover up the body of Curley's wife in the same way that he tried earlier to cover up the body of the puppy. When he flees, he takes the dead, soft puppy with him.

Candy finds the dead body when he comes to tell Lennie something about tending the rabbits in their dream place, and immediately upon seeing the body, Candy knows that this is the end of the dream. He runs to George, hoping that just the two of them can still fulfill the dream. Throughout this conversation between George and Candy, it is never mentioned that Lennie killed the woman, but both know that he did. George now sees himself as one of the lonely people who will "take my fifty bucks an . . . stay all night in some lousy cat house . . . or set in some poolroom. . . ." This motif then carries the reader back to the opening chapter when George was complaining that he never got to do these things. Now George can do them and there is a note of pathos about his freedom because it is not really freedom but a life now of loneliness and desperation.

Almost paternally, George is determined that no one be allowed to hurt Lennie. He asks Candy to delay before telling the others, explaining that he wants no suspicion cast on him, but in reality, he wants the opportunity to steal Carlson's gun. Thus, even now, George knows immediately what he must do and makes preparations for it. Handily, if old Candy's dog had not needed to be killed George would not have known of the gun, and if the dog had not been killed, old Candy would not have become a part of the group and would not have helped George in the manner in which he did. Consequently, the death of Candy's old dog now assumes added importance in the final action of the novel.

After George leaves, note that old Candy again recalls the lost dream and curses Curley's wife for its loss. The repetition of the dream now rises to a higher degree of pathos, since it is irrevocably lost.

Curley's viciousness and determination for revenge is motivated partly by his hatred for Lennie, who crushed his hand. The fierce hatred convinces George that he must kill Lennie himself rather than watch his friend be mutilated by Curley.

CHAPTER SIX

Summary

By the side of the pool where the waters move peacefully, Lennie kneels down and takes a long drink of water. He is very proud of himself because he did not forget to return to this secret, safe place just as George had told him to do.

While he is sitting, a huge apparition of his aunt appears and scolds him for not being a nice boy and for causing George so much trouble. She reminds Lennie of how much fun George could have had if he had not spent all this time looking after him. Lennie feels bad about this, and wonders if he can still tend the rabbits.

Then, suddenly, Aunt Clara disappears and a huge rabbit appears and scornfully tells Lennie that he is not fit to tend to rabbits because he would let them all starve. The rabbit warns Lennie that George is going to beat "hell outa you with a stick," but Lennie is sure that George won't be cruel to him. The rabbit says that George is going to leave Lennie now, but the man-boy can hear no more and puts his hands over his ears. He wails loudly for George.

Seconds later, George does appear and tells Lennie to be quiet. When Lennie tells George that he has done another bad thing, George tells him that it makes no difference. Lennie waits for George to get angry and "give him hell"; but George doesn't say anything except everything will be all right.

Lennie asks George to tell about the farm that they are going to get and to tell how he and George will be different from the other guys. George begins once again to tell about their future plans. He stops, however, in the middle of the narration and listens to the approaching sounds. Then he tells Lennie to look across the stream and try to visualize the place they are going to get. George recalls the rabbits which Lennie will get to tend and assures Lennie that they will be in a place where no one can hurt them. Lennie is still staring across the river, and becoming so excited about their place that he wants to go to it immediately. George agrees and slowly lifts the pistol and fires it into the back of Lennie's head. His companion falls over into the sand.

Curley and the group of farmhands burst through the brush and are surprised to find that George has killed Lennie. Slim goes over to George and assures him that it was something a guy just had to do. He wants to take George out for a drink, and as they leave he tells George "You hadda, George, I swear you hadda." Curley and the other farmhands do not understand why George and Slim are leaving.

Commentary

The novel opened with the quiet and peace of the riverside, and now at its close, we return to the same setting for the last chapter. In the meantime, we have seen the deaths of an old dog, a young puppy, and a young woman. The sense of quietness then is modified by this knowledge.

Lennie is very proud of himself for remembering to come back to this place. He knows that he has done a bad thing, but only associates it with something like asking for ketchup when there isn't any. He knows that George will be angry, and thinks that he should go off somewhere and live by himself. In other words, Lennie is essentially reliving many of the arguments that they have had in the past, and makes no direct evaluation of the degree of seriousness involved in his murdering Curley's wife.

Lennie has great faith in George and when the apparition of his Aunt Clara or the giant rabbit appears, he defends his friend George and asserts with authority that George "ain't gonna be mean." George, however, will kill his friend Lennie in a few minutes, demonstrating in an ironic way that Lennie is right because this is the kindest thing he can do for Lennie.

When George arrives, there is a sad air of defeatism about him. He knows the task that is facing him and does not have the strength to scold Lennie for anything. It is ironic that Lennie can remember most of the things that George has said about their relationship, but nothing else. Thus, he forces George to repeat his old complaint about having to tend to Lennie and not having the opportunity to go to the cat house, etc. The pathos here is that in a few minutes, George *will* be free and will go with Slim for a drink, but he will be entirely alone.

In the preceding chapter, when Lennie killed Curley's wife, the emphasis of the narration was on Lennie. Now, as George is about to kill Lennie, note that the emphasis is focused on George. He has been compelled once again to recapitulate the dream of the place they are going to have someday, and as he does so, he concludes with the statement that no one will be able to hurt Lennie. Lennie wants to go immediately, thus George must now kill him, especially since the other men are getting nearer. Thus, Lennie dies in happiness thinking only of the dream place. George, however, now must face the miserable life and existence of a man who has no one to care for and a life in which no one cares for him. But in the same way that it was earlier necessary and best to kill the old dog, so was it necessary for George to kill Lennie. Only Slim is able to perceive this fact, and tries to comfort George by taking him away "to get a drink." George goes knowing that now he is free to go off drinking at any time he wants to.

GENERAL MEANING

Steinbeck has often been considered a writer who concerns himself with a social message in his novels. While this view may be partially correct, it in no way indicates the mastery with which Steinbeck explores a human predicament with warmth and compassion. Steinbeck's main concern in *Of Mice and Men* lies in his compassion for the below-average, the downtrodden, and the dispossessed. Steinbeck had seen the type of men depicted in this novel, had seen them hurt and lonely, and he wished to convey his feelings to others by creating a simple, objective, but compassionate picture of this type. He wanted a large audience of readers to come to an understanding of a class of people far different from the average reader. George, Lennie, Candy, Slim—this type would never read a novel, but a modern novel about these people could help countless numbers of readers understand this sort of man. Consequently, this novel, along with much of Steinbeck's writing, attempts to achieve a broader understanding among various members of mankind.

This drive for understanding between peoples is not a direct theme of this novel, but the general aim of Steinbeck's entire work. More specifically, in *Of Mice and Men* he asks for the right of all men to create and strive after their own individual dreams. However lowly on the social ladder Lennie and George may be, they still possess that inalienable human right to pursue their individual dreams. George and Lennie's vision of a place of their own where they can live "off the fatta the lan'," can have rabbits, and can be protected from hurt becomes the focal point of the story. As the two protagonists speculate about their dreams for the future, Candy, Crooks, and even Curley's wife reveal that they also have dreams, also have visions of a life far different from their present one.

If Steinbeck were only the social critic, he would have presented each of his characters being defeated by forces of society. Instead, he shows that each character is ultimately destroyed by his own limitation. The tragedy lies not in society but in the individual flaws inherent in each personality. George, the central spokesman, trusts Lennie too much and, as a result, Lennie kills both Curley's wife and George's dream at the same time. In contrast, even though Lennie's dream is never realized, he died believing in it. Curley's wife died because part of her dream involved being well liked, and when she attempts to make friends with Lennie, she goes too far and is killed.

Another central theme embodied in this work is the need and desire for comradeship. Steinbeck is concerned with showing the value of and the need for friendship. Man is seemingly not created for a lonely and isolated life, and craves some type of communication with his fellow man. The need for social companionship is a basic urge common to all men and deserves consideration as a fundamental aspect of life.

The relationship between George and Lennie is unique in that the stray farmhand is usually an isolated person. It is emphasized repeatedly throughout the novel that two workers are virtually never seen together. Lennie and George have an attachment and under-standing between them; their relationship is different and valuable. It becomes an integral part of their dream and vision that while other people have no one, they do have each other and consequently can look after each other. Their basic relationship is seen then to be the initiating factor in their dream which always begins the narra-tion: "Guys like us, that work on ranches, are the loneliest guys in the world. They got no fambly. They don't belong no place.... With us it ain't like that. We got a future. We got somebody to talk to that gives a damn about us...."

Consequently, two central ideas are correlated in Lennie and George's companionship and in their dreams of the future. The tragedy of the novel is that the two are so perfectly connected that when one is destroyed the other is automatically destroyed.

The theme of loneliness is depicted in multiple ways throughout the novel. Old Candy has only his dog and when it is killed, he hears of George and Lennie's dream, and attaches himself to them so that he won't end up someday totally alone and an outcast. Even after Lennie kills Curley's wife, old Candy still wants to join George and carry out the dream. Likewise, Crooks, the Negro stable hand, is pathetically revealed to be on the verge of destruction because "a guy needs somebody—to be near him.... A guy goes nuts if he ain't got nobody. Don't make no difference who the guy is, long's he with you. I tell ye...a guy gets too lonely an' he gets sick." Crooks then would be willing to come to the farm and work for nothing just to have the opportunity of communicating with people.

Curley's wife ultimately is one of the loneliest people in the novel. Her behavior is at times so detestable that one cannot become very sympathetic, but nevertheless, she makes herself so unpleasant because she too is compelled by her loneliness: "Think I don't like to talk to somebody ever' once in a while?" She is so overwhelmed by her total isolation that she can only bewail her predicament as follows: "Sat'iday night...an' what am I doin'? Standin' here talkin' to a bunch of bindle stiffs—a nigger an' a dum-dum and a lousy ol' sheep—an' liking it because they ain't nobody else." In spite of her intentional insult, she is perhaps the most pathetic character in the novel. She seeks out Lennie's friendship because the other men fear Curley and will have nothing to do with her. Thus, the loneliest person in the novel becomes the cause of the destruction of George and Lennie's comradeship.

The ultimate value of the friendship between George and Lennie becomes the focal point of the novel. If this relationship did not exist, then the final act of killing Lennie would not possess the overtones of tragedy because now George's life will become as lonely and as frustrated as were the lives of the other characters.

Steinbeck has thus combined two highly important aspects of human nature into one inextricable presentation. The ability of man to dream must rely directly upon having someone to share that dream with.

CHARACTER ANALYSES

GEORGE MILTON

George is a little man physically, but he possesses a certain degree of largeness. He is described as a small, quick, restless man who is distinguished by sharp features. He moves quickly and adroitly, and thinks a thing through before acting. In terms of the entire novel, he stands in diametric contrast to his large, clumsy companion. Outwardly, George seems to be an angry man who is disgusted at having to care for his simpleminded companion. He grew up in the same town as did Lennie, and when Lennie's Aunt Clara died, Lennie and George started wandering around together like two stray dogs.

George's nature is such that he must constantly complain about the amount of trouble that Lennie causes him. This is clearly illustrated in the first part of the novel when George mentions all the things that he could do if he did not have to watch after Lennie. He complains that he never gets to go to a "cat house" or to the poolroom or do the other things that workers do. It is soon revealed that George has made this complaint so often that it has become a part of their life together.

George often makes the complaint partly because he does get annoyed at his large and simpleminded friend, but also, partly because he is the type of person who must complain as a point of general principle. From the early pages of the novel, the superficial first impression is that George is harsh with Lennie, but in terms of the entire novel, we might say that he was, if anything, not strict enough.

George has, however—as if to counter his constant griping—created a dream of their having a place someday. The crux of the dream seems to be that once there, no one can harm Lennie. It will be a safe place, a lair for him. George, then, is anxious to secure his own place so that Lennie can live the type of life where he can be happy and will not be hurt by people who don't understand his simple ways.

Thus, ultimately, in spite of the way that George talks and complains, we should see that he has a strong protective feeling about his big companion. Most of the things he does are for Lennie's sake or to protect Lennie. For example, he hides in a ditch filled with water in order to protect Lennie from a posse; he sleeps in the open field so that Lennie will not have to arrive at the farm at the wrong time; he gets Lennie a puppy; and finally, he kills Lennie so that the misfit will not be brutally destroyed by the vicious Curley.

George knows that even though Lennie commits some acts that are bad in the eyes of society, yet Lennie himself is not cruel. The system of judgment used by George seems to be that of judging a man as to whether he is brutal or not. When George takes something away from Lennie, he explains that he is not being intentionally mean, but is doing the thing for Lennie's own good. In contrast, he knows that Curley is, by nature, a fighter and is frightened of what a man like Curley can do. Thus, whenever Lennie commits some "bad" act, George is the first to assert that it was *not* committed out of meanness. Even George, however, cannot ignore the magnitude of the final crime committed by Lennie.

Lennie's tragedy is not isolated from George's personal sense of the tragic; that is, George had earlier emphasized often in his conversation with Lennie that the two of them were different from other people, because others have no one who cares for them. Lennie and George have each other. Thus, when he has to destroy his companion at the end of the novel, George is ironically free to do all the things he had earlier complained that he couldn't do. But by now, the reader knows that George will become in essence a living dead man because he has no friend and no comrade to communicate with.

LENNIE SMALL

Even though Lennie's last name is Small, he is, physically, just the opposite: a giant of a man with prodigious strength having the power to kill. This large man also contrasts with his smaller companion, George, who looks after him. Ironically, then, the small man is the keeper of the larger Lennie Small.

Lennie is the antithesis to George in several other ways. He is very slow and clumsy; he can remember nothing except the things which George says; he is frightened of people and avoids them; and, he is content as long as he has George to look after him.

The basic response that the reader has for Lennie is conditioned by the simple childlike manner in which Lennie does and sees things. In the first chapter, he delights in making the water ripple, and he is content to pet a dead mouse. His pleasures are those of the innocent and naive child, and it is this quality which characterizes his every action in the novel. Steinbeck uses the episode of petting the dead mouse early in the novel so as to elicit a sympathetic response for this simpleminded man. Basically, society would not condone such an act as petting a mouse dead or alive and more especially a dead one. Yet Lennie's desire to pet this dead rodent is an indication of his basic simplicity. He sees nothing wrong with the act because he does not function in terms of the dictates set up by society. Consequently, we must judge him by relative standards rather than the absolute ones of normal society.

Lennie, himself, is often compared to an animal. His responses to life are those of a simple animal. Like a pet dog, he gives his complete devotion to his friend George, and the image of him fetching the dead mouse to George is similar to that of a dog fetching a stick to its master. This analogy is carried further when we discover that Lennie responds to the voice and words of his master, but does not remember past events. Lennie has completely forgotten the trouble he got into in the last town, but he can remember almost everything that George says. He, then, is trained to responses in life by George's voice, and acts mainly upon this voice command. This is aptly illustrated in the fight between Lennie and Curley. Lennie knew that George had told him not to fight and not to cause trouble; therefore, he merely cowered while Curley hit him, but when George gave the command for Lennies to hit back, the big man simply reached out and crushed the smaller Curley.

Lennie's basic animal nature allows him to follow commands of work; consequently, it is his hulking strength which gets and secures jobs for them because he can be shown how to do a heavy job and will continue to work until told to stop. In further contrast to these tremendous physical feats is his innate love for little things, especially furry rabbits. Lennie's dream is to have all the rabbits that he can take care of, and his attempts to do the right thing are motivated by his fear that George won't let him take care of the rabbits.

Lennie's greatest difficulty is in *remembering*. While he never plans to do anything wrong, he simply can't remember what is wrong and what is not. This idea is repeated many times during the novel by Steinbeck's mentioning how often Lennie forgets that little animals must be treated gently. In the climactic scene in the barn, Lennie has just been playing with his small puppy and accidentally killed it. He could not remember to treat it gently. When Curley's wife appears and allows Lennie to stroke her hair, he could not remember to stroke softly and could not remember the terror of his own strength and accidentally killed her in the same simple manner that he had killed the little animals that he loved.

The question arises as to how Lennie can forget everything else but still remember to return to the place that George pointed out. The point is that Lennie, like a trained animal, does remember most of the things that George tells him. For example, he can remember the entire narration about their dream place, and he can remember what George says when he is angry. Thus, since George instructed him to return to a certain place, Lennie does remember this thing. One should also remember that an animal has an instinctive knowledge of hiding places. The bushes by the stream where the rabbits fled are the spot that Lennie also scampers to during danger.

If Lennie is so dependent upon George for his very existence, what would happen if George left Lennie? It is now apparent that Lennie is helpless without his friend. George would be willing to allow Lennie to be locked up somewhere after the death of Curley's wife, but Curley is determined to brutally kill Lennie. Thus, as Carlson had to kill the old dog, George kills Lennie because Lennie would have become too confused and too terrified if others tried to track him down like an animal.

SLIM

Slim plays a very minor but necessary role in the novel. There is a need for the objective and strong voice of rationalism and a need for a sympathetic friend. Slim is the type which evokes confidences but does not demand them. Thus, George feels quite free in talking with this man and explains Lennie's behavior to him. Slim has observed Lennie and agrees that Lennie might be simple but there is nothing mean about him.

Slim also functions to act as an intermediary when Lennie and Curley fight. His calm control of the situation suggests a mature appreciation of the difficulties which George faces. Finally, at the end of the novel, Slim is the only person who understands George's motivation, and he tries to sympathize with George. He is, then, the sympathetic listener who understands more fully George's predicament than do any of the other farmhands.

CURLEY

Early in the novel, George must take away a mouse from Lennie; he explains that he is not being mean when he does so. Later when George explains some of Lennie's erratic acts, he emphasizes over and over that Lennie has never done anything that one could consider mean. Even when Carlson kills old Candy's blind dog, he does not do so out of meanness.

As a contrast to the above, we have the character of Curley who represents the lowest type of meanness. Curley is physically a little person who likes to get into fights with larger people. If he wins the fight, he is thought to be a "game" little fighter. But if he loses, then everyone says that the bigger person should not have fought with the little person. As Candy says: "Seems like Curley ain't givin' nobody a chance." In a sense, this is what happens between Curley and Lennie. The little guy jumps on the bigger person and begins beating him. Then, when Lennie crushes Curley's hand, Curley develops a hatred for the bigger man which will be expressed in his desire to mutilate Lennie in the final scene.

Curley's meanness causes him to leave his wife alone most of the time but he demands that she not talk to the farmhands. By imposing this isolation on her, he causes her to seek available company, even in the form of the retarded Lennie. Ultimately then, Curley's meanness functions as a direct contrast to the simple Lennie's desire to love and pet almost everything.

STRUCTURE

Steinbeck uses essentially a dramatic structure for this novel. He wanted to write a work of fiction which resembled a drama as much as possible. The simplest way of seeing this structure is to examine the setting in each scene. Often, in any given scene in fiction, the characters can easily wander around from one place to another, but in this novel, each scene is confined to one small area where the entire action of that scene is enacted.

The dramatic structure is further demonstrated by the fact that Steinbeck adapted the novel almost intact for the stage in 1937, where it became a successful drama. Compare the novel with the synopsis of the scenes found in the dramatic work:

ACT I
Scene i. A sandy bank of the Salinas River.
Scene ii. The interior of a bunkhouse.

ACT II
Scene i. The same as Act I, scene ii.
Scene ii. The room of the stable buck, a lean-to.

ACT III
Scene i. One end of a great barn.
Scene ii. Same as Act I, scene i.

Much of the novel is in dialogue which has also been transferred almost verbatim to the stage. The structure, then, relies upon an almost total objectification of the feelings of the characters. To do this Steinbeck opens and closes his novel at a scene by the river. In these scenes, we see into the true nature of the two companions. The central portion of the novel takes place in the environs of the farm—the bunkhouse, the stable room, and the barn. In these middle scenes, we see the main characters in relationship to other people.

Therefore, in the first scene, the dreams, the desires, and the personalities of Lennie and George are presented. Through the next four scenes, we watch these aspects against a social milieu and observe their modifications. The last scene shows the inevitable destruction of these earlier traits and visions.

STYLE

On a first reading, Steinbeck's prose appears to lack distinction because of its complete and total naturalness. Nothing is much more difficult to achieve than an appearance of utter simplicity. Part of Steinbeck's greatness lies in his ability to capture this tone of basic reality. His ability to write a type of dialogue which never has a false note in it is a part of this achievement. The natural quality of the dialogue may be seen by comparing the number of speeches taken verbatim from the novel and utilized in the play.

To achieve simplicity in style is not easy, nor is all of Steinbeck's writing aimed at this effect. Many of his sentences employ such tradi-tional devices as balance and antithesis, parallelism, alliteration, and repetition. Other sentences, especially descriptive ones, achieve a rhymthic quality reminiscent of Biblical poetry. The following sentence from the opening paragraph uses parallelisms and repetition effectively. "Rabbits come out of the brush to sit on the sand in the evening, and the damp flats are covered with the night tracks of 'coons, and with the spread pads of dogs from the ranches, and with the split wedge tracks of deer that come to drink in the dark." The language in this sentence is quite simple, but moves from one repetition to another, repeating the phrase "with the...."

The second paragraph possesses a high rhymthic flow and could be converted into free verse:

> "There is a path through the willows and among
> the sycamores,

> A path beaten hard by boys coming down from the
>   ranches to swim in the deep pool,
> And beaten hard by tramps who come wearily down
>   from the highway."

Steinbeck also uses such poetic techniques as the *simile* to introduce some of his motifs: "On the sand banks the rabbits sat as quietly as little gray sculptured stones." Numerous other examples could be found to illustrate other techniques, but the important thing to remember is that Steinbeck's style is always functional. He never describes anything unless it will serve as support of his story, and he keeps his dialogue and narrative as simple as possible so as to blend in with the simplicity of his subject matter.

QUESTIONS FOR REVIEW

1. How does Steinbeck make the reader sympathetic toward Lennie?

2. Discuss Steinbeck's use of irony.

3. Why is Curley's wife never given a personal name?

4. Analyze the style of the novel, comparing and contrasting descriptive passages with passages of dialogue.

5. Why does George emphasize "meanness" as a central quality for judging people?

6. How does the death of Candy's old, blind dog function in relationship to the central theme of the novel?

7. Discuss the value of such a relationship as that between George and Lennie.

8. What is the purpose of having Crooks be a Negro? Does this fact heighten the theme of loneliness?

9. Distinguish between the *tragic* and the *pathetic* in the novel.

10. Discuss the relationship between man's dream and his social situation.

SELECTED BIBLIOGRAPHY

Fontenrose, Joseph. *John Steinbeck: An Introduction and Interpretation*. New York: 1963.

French, Warren. *John Steinbeck*. New York: Twayne, 1961.

Lisca, Peter. *The Wide World of John Steinbeck*. New Brunswick: Rutgers University Press, 1958.

Moore, Harry T. *The Novels of John Steinbeck: A First Critical Study*. Chicago: Normandie House, 1939.

Tedlock, E. W. Jr., and Wicker, C. V., eds. *Steinbeck and His Critics: A Record of Twenty-Five Years*. Albuquerque: University of New Mexico Press, 1957.

Watt, F. W. *John Steinbeck*. New York: Grove Press, 1962

LIST OF STEINBECK'S WORKS

1929 *Cup of Gold*

1932 *The Pastures of Heaven*

1933 *To a God Unknown*
      The Red Pony (filmed in 1949)

1934 "The Murder" (an O. Henry prize short story, 1934)

1935 *Tortilla Flat* (Commonwealth Club of California Gold Medal and filmed during the forties)

1936 *In Dubious Battle*

1937 *Of Mice and Men* (novel, play and later a film)

1938 *The Long Valley* (short story collection)

1939 *The Grapes of Wrath* (Pulitzer Prize and later filmed)

1941 *The Sea of Cortez: A Leisurely Journal of Travel and Research*
The Forgotten Village (semi-documentary Mexican film)

1942 *Bombs Away: The Story of a Bomber Team*
The Moon Is Down (play-novella and later a film)

1945 *Cannery Row*

1947 *The Wayward Bus* (novel and later a film)
The Pearl (novella and later a film)

1948 *A Russian Journal*

1950 *Burning Bright* (novella and play)
Viva Zapata (film)

1951 *The Log From the Sea of Cortez* (the narrative portion of
Sea of Cortez with a tribute "About Ed Ricketts")

1952 *East of Eden* (novel and later a film)

1954 *Sweet Thursday* (novel and later a Rodgers and Hammerstein
musical comedy, *Pipe Dream*)

1959 *Once There Was a War*

1961 *The Winter of Our Discontent*

1962 *Travels with Charley in Search of America*

NOTES

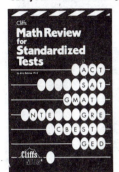

Your Guides to Successful Test Preparation.

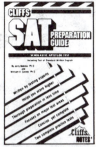  

Cliffs Test Preparation Guides

Efficient preparation means better test scores. Go with the experts and use **Cliffs Test Preparation Guides.** They'll help you reach your goals because they're: Complete • Concise • Functional • In-depth. They are focused on helping you know what to expect from each test. The test-taking techniques have been proven in classroom programs nationwide.

Recommended for individual use or as a part of formal test preparation programs.

TITLES		QTY.
2068-8	**ENHANCED ACT ($5.95)**	
2030-0	**CBEST ($7.95)**	
2040-8	**CLAST ($8.95)**	
1471-8	**ESSAY EXAM ($4.95)**	
2031-9	**ELM Review ($6.95)**	
2060-2	**GMAT ($7.95)**	
2008-4	**GRE ($6.95)**	
2065-3	**LSAT ($7.95)**	
2033-5	**MATH Review for Standardized Tests ($8.95)**	
2017-3	**NTE Core Battery ($14.95)**	
2020-3	**Memory Power for Exams ($4.95)**	
2044-0	**Police Sergeant Examination Preparation Guide ($9.95)**	
2032-7	**PPST ($7.95)**	
2002-5	**PSAT/NMSQT ($4.50)**	
2000-9	**SAT ($5.95)**	
2042-4	**TASP ($7.95)**	
2018-1	**TOEFL w/cassette ($14.95)**	
2034-3	**VERBAL Review for Standardized Tests ($7.95)**	
2041-6	**You Can Pass the GED ($9.95)**	

Prices subject to change without notice.

Available at your local bookseller or order by sending the coupon with your check. **Cliffs Notes, Inc., P.O. Box 80728, Lincoln, NE 68501.**

Name _____

Address _____

City _____

State _____ **Zip**_____

P.O. Box 80728, Lincoln, NE 68501

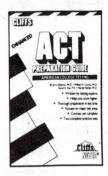
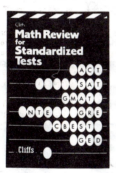

LET CLIFFS NOTES

GET B   D
WIT

813.
52
STEINBECK

$3.75

Carey, Gary

Of mice and men : notes

DUE DATE		0046 4892	
3-7/13